Pick Up Your Cross and Follow Me

Volume I of the N.E.M. Discipleship Series

Dcn. Ralph Poyo

ISBN: 0-9850-2560-3
ISBN-13: 9780985025601

Authors Note

Who is this book for? This material is for anyone who wants to become a mature Disciple of Jesus Christ. My hope is that it will be particularly helpful for faithful Catholics who have recently experienced a conversion; they have gone beyond the "rules" of our faith and have encountered Jesus in their hearts – through the power of the Holy Spirit.

Literary Form – In the first edition I attempted to use a gender neutral method for acknowledging Disciples of Christ as both men and women. Many readers found this approach confusing and awkward. For simplicity, I decided to use the traditional use of the pronoun "he" not to be exclusionary but to avoid awkward phrasing.

Table of Contents

Acknowledgments

I praise God for the guidance of Mother Mary and the Holy Spirit in learning how to lead hearts to Jesus.

ᚥ᙮ᚥ

I am very thankful for my wife, Susan, who is a constant source of support, encouragement, and love.

ᚥ᙮ᚥ

I am so blessed by my daughters—Sarah, Rachel, Leah, Rebekah, Hannah—and son-in-law, Russell Hoyt, who have humbly worked in their own way to help me serve the Lord.

ᚥ᙮ᚥ

Special thanks for the prayer warriors who support New Evangelization Ministries (NEM). They fight when no one is watching.

ᚥ᙮ᚥ

Very special thanks to my dear friend, prayer warrior, and fellow servant of NEM, Elisa Wern.

ᚥ᙮ᚥ

Thanks to my brother, Bob Poyo, and Marianne Kersey for the hours of time spent editing this material.

Goals

The Goal of Evangelization

The ultimate goal of evangelization is to bring people into intimate relationship with Jesus Christ, through the Holy Spirit, and welcome them into the Church.

Having heard the gospel message, a person drawn by the Holy Spirit is moved to respond to His promptings of his own free will. As he recognizes Jesus' love shown through His death on the cross, His sacrificial act becomes more personal to him. He realizes first that Jesus died for *him* and then the magnitude of His sacrifice. Because Christ's love touches the heart, increasingly a person feels a need to respond to this love. This is a pivotal moment when he freely makes the choice to give his life to Jesus. If that person is you, congratulations!

This gift of self requires an essential element—repentance. A believer in Christ must no longer desire to be in control, making all the decisions as if he were God. He must choose to pursue a relationship with Jesus, placing Him above everything else in life and yielding to Christ (who is God) in humility. Once a person has arrived at this point, he must also choose to participate in the outward sign of baptism. This is a public testimony of commitment to the inward sign of dying to self and living his life for Jesus.

New believers who were baptized as infants must now intentionally choose to give their lives to Jesus by ratifying the choice their parents made for them as children.

At baptism, a person receives the indwelling of the Holy Spirit, which creates the opportunity for an intimate relationship, or union, with Christ. A time of growth is needed in this new relationship so trust can be established between the believer and the Lord. When this relationship with Christ has been achieved, the person's spiritual journey and the intimate union with Christ will be empowered by the Holy Spirit.

When the person is ready, the Holy Spirit's revelation of Christ's presence in the heart of the believer is expressed by a manifestation of the fruits of the Holy Spirit: love, joy, peace, patience, kindness, generosity, faithfulness, gentleness, and self-control (Galatians 5:22-23). Progressively, new believers become disciples, students or followers, of Christ. They begin learning to live their lives in a new way, in faith and hope that Jesus will ultimately lead them to be with God the Father face to face, which is called the beatific vision.

The Goal of Discipleship
The goal of a disciple is to mature in the spiritual disciplines that enable him to grow deeper in love with

each person of the Holy Trinity (God the Father, Jesus, and the Holy Spirit) and the Church. As this love grows and matures, a disciple becomes increasingly selfless, giving more of himself to Christ and others. The result is the flowing of The Holy Spirit through his heart, mind and actions for the benefit of others.

Like a newborn baby, a person declaring himself for Jesus is defenseless and fragile. The enemy, actively operating through the world and our weakened flesh, has been constantly working to keep him away from God. Although God's grace is far stronger than the power of the enemy and his fallen angels, the new disciple must cooperate with the grace of God in fighting the enemy's direct attacks. If he focuses his efforts and grows closer to Jesus, the power of His grace and presence will be made evident in his life.

Satan and his evil spirits will continue to fight angrily to keep the new disciple from developing a relationship with Jesus Christ. Every new disciple must fight forces of evil that have entrenched him in his habits, thoughts, words, deeds, and understanding (knowledge). No disciple by himself can be victorious over the enemy's attacks. While the Lord allows it to be a difficult fight, He uses the struggle to train disciples to learn to depend on His assistance. Each disciple must fight to know, love, and serve God. God's holy will must be desired above everything, especially the disciple's own will. You must never let go of your relationship with Christ. If the enemy is victorious in severing your relationship through sin, be encouraged that God provides a way for you to reestablish this relationship— through the Sacrament of Reconciliation.

At the inception of the Church, the Holy Spirit revealed to the apostles four spiritual disciplines needed for growth: the apostles' teaching (Scripture study), the sacramental life (breaking of the Bread), community (life in Christ), and prayer (personal and communal prayer life) (Acts 2:42). All disciples must be firmly rooted in each of these disciplines for them to grow and flourish in their lives and service for the Lord.

The School of the Holy Spirit

The Holy Spirit is the guide given to you at baptism for the specific purpose of completing the good work He began in you (Philippians 1:6). You will grow closer to Christ by getting to know the one He sent you, the Holy Spirit. Learn to listen to Him. Be patient, persistent, and available. He speaks often to those who desire first and foremost to do His will.

Each day, invite the Holy Spirits presence, guidance and grace into everything you do. Ask the Spirit to help you grow in your faith. And ask Him for a plan to grow in your disciplines. Be sure it is reasonable, doable, and measureable; it must be one that you can realistically accomplish. Incremental steps of action will help you progress and grow. Run your new plan by a priest or other mature disciple to make sure it is feasible. Watch for it to bear good fruit.

From the moment you wake, ask Him to be involved in your day. When you eat, thank Him for your meals and other provisions. When you work, ask for His help with each task. When you meet with others, ask Him to bless them and the time spent together. When you pray and study Scripture, ask the Holy Spirit to reveal the truths He has for you, and for the grace and courage to live it. By inviting the Spirit to be an active participant in the things you do, you will infuse God into every part of your life.

Jesus told Nicodemus that he must be born again to enter the kingdom of God. The conversion experience Jesus was speaking of occurs when your spirit is regenerated through intimate union with the Holy Spirit. As the Holy Spirit dwells in your heart, the fruit of the Spirit becomes evident in your life. To be born again, then, is to have the Holy Spirit come alive in you to the point that His presence becomes increasingly apparent in all your actions. Without the Spirit's visible presence, you are simply going through the motions of church behavior as a learned response. Remember, all that you do should come from this union with God.

ॐ∾ॐ

Living as Part of the Body of Christ

It is vital that new disciples be involved in some sort of spiritual development group at Church. They need consistent contact with other disciples who provide support and accountability to help protect the newfound relationship with Christ. *The number one reason people give up on their relationship with Jesus is that they try to develop this relationship alone.* God uses Mother Church to care for and protect her young. He designed His Church to be a community of believers.

Every disciple of Christ must understand that their conversion and baptism are the beginning of a lifelong journey. As a disciple grows and matures, he will look for opportunities to help others establish and grow in their relationship with Christ. Discipleship has *everything* to do with walking in the Spirit with others. When you are ready, the Spirit will begin to use you.

The Holy Spirit helps disciples understand that their life is no longer about themselves, but about Jesus and their personal relationship with Him. This new perspective is a natural fruit of the conversion experience.

It enables us to experience a love greater than any other, the love of God.

> As God's love grows within your heart, your desire for Jesus' life to be intertwined with yours will also grow.

When this occurs, the disciple responds to Christ's love with a desire to serve others. The disciple who comes to love Jesus and live for Him realizes that he is no longer an individual, but is now joined with Jesus as part of His family.

> You are now united to others through your mutual love for Jesus and the presence of the Holy Spirit within each family member.

A genuine disciple pursues opportunities to gather with others who are also seeking and serving Christ. Like a hot coal in a fire, you will continue to glow as long as you remain close to others who are also on fire. Move away, and you will grow cold and lose your spiritual life.

Satan and his army tempt disciples with aspects of their previous life. First, they strive to get you to return to your old way of living where there was no desire, time, or room for God or church activities. Second, they try to have you believe that your previous priorities are still relevant and should take precedence over your new spiritual desires.

The disciple's life should now be focused on growing closer to Jesus. As a disciple, you need to be involved in activities where you can gather with others to (1) grow in faith, (2) worship God, and (3) serve others.

As you progress in your journey, ask the Holy Spirit to lead you to a group who will lead you to keep the fire of faith alive.

Additionally, a disciple should always be prepared to share the gifts God gave him whenever the Holy Spirit prompts him. A disciple is always looking for opportunities to connect others to Jesus.

If you aren't sure what your gifts are, find a disciple further along in the journey to guide you.

Prayer

A disciple of Jesus Christ must take time away from ministry and work to be with God, his Father. He must commit a consistent time each day to spend with God—ideally the most productive time of his day. Some dedicate a place for prayer (such as sitting in a chair or at a table, with a cross to reflect on and a picture of Mary); others devote an entire room to prayer.

Prayer is conversation with God, and allowing time to listen to what God wants to say to you is important. Your spiritual growth occurs as a result of being in a relationship with Jesus, a relationship that requires communication..

Begin with fifteen or twenty minutes a day—*every* day. If you miss a day, get back on track as soon as possible. Divide the time into parts. Use part of the time to invite God to join you, tell Him your concerns, and pray for others. Spend another part of the time reading Scripture (more on this later), and finally, set aside time to listen to God.

Warning: Satan and his demons will focus on disrupting or interrupting your prayer time. Distractions will come. Keeping you from effective prayer separates you from God, and that is the enemy's ultimate goal.

It is often helpful for believers working toward establishing a consistent prayer habit to use the acronym ACTS as a guide:

A = Adoration—Spend time adoring, or praising, God.
C = Confession—Examine your conscience and ask God to forgive your sins.
T = Thanksgiving—Give God thanks for all your blessings.
S = Supplication—Pray for your needs and the needs of others.

Always end your quiet time with a period of silence in which you patiently listen for God to speak. Prayer is a time of communication with God, and it is important to allow God His opportunity to speak.

A disciple must often sacrifice much and put personal wants and desires after his chief objective—in this case, time with God. This is the process of *dying to self* (putting God first) and is among the most challenging commitments you will ever make.

The Habit of Prayer

First, setting aside consistent time for prayer requires a strong commitment. Satan, the king of lies, attempts to convince disciples that they do not have time for prayer. He does anything to keep them from quality time with God.

Trust that Jesus wants to spend time in prayer with you and will provide the time to accomplish this (and everything He needs you to do each day).

As with any commitment, this requires you to make choices to change your normal behavior, habits, or attitudes (for example, sleep a little less, watch less TV, or value the importance of prayer).

Second, as a disciple perseveres and tries to settle into an effective prayer routine, Satan does everything possible to distract him, both in efforts to pray and while actually praying.

Be aware. Satan can place thoughts in your mind, though he cannot read or hear your thoughts (God keeps that gift to himself for silent prayer). When this happens, take each distracting thought and pray aloud about it. For example, you may say one or a series of things like, "Lord, I lift up my bills. Please take care of my sister/ brother/daughter/son. Give my wife/husband time to prepare for work. Help me to be still in prayer." *When Satan sees his distracting thoughts being turned into prayer, he either ceases or his efforts or greatly diminishes them.*

Third, another challenge is Satan trying to make you believe that your prayers are not accomplishing anything because fruit of the Spirit is not yet visible in your life or you are not hearing God talk to you.

Remember, you are developing a habit. The goal of this habit is to devote quality time with God consistently into a life where it has never existed. It will take time. God wants it as much as you do—if not more—and doing it requires patience and persistence.

Fourth, once prayer becomes a virtue, you may find your heart desiring more time with the Lord. As the Spirit leads, increase your prayer time. Remember, your destiny is to be with the Lord and you need to practice being with Him.

A word of caution: A common mistake many believers make when first establishing a prayer time or routine is to set unrealistic expectations and create unreachable goals. Satan is quick to exploit this, causing the disciple to become discouraged and quit.

Note that an important component of your prayer life is Scripture study during prayer time. The key is to learn how to listen to God as he speaks to you through the Scriptures you will be studying.

෨෧

Scripture Study

Every disciple of Christ must become a student of the Word. The love we experience in our conversion instills a desire to know Christ, to grow closer to Him, and to spend time in His presence. This is why God gave us the Bible. It is the *Word* of God. The Bible gives us access to God and knowledge of Him anytime we want.

St. Jerome said, "Ignorance of Scripture is ignorance of Christ." *(Commentariorum in Isaiam libri xviii prol.:PL 24,17B.)* To study Scripture is to be tutored by the Holy Spirit. St. Paul described the Scriptures as the sword of the Holy Spirit (Ephesians 6).

Clearly, getting familiar with the Bible is very important. As a disciple, you must first learn what the sword is before you can wield it. I encourage you to get a Catholic Study Bible. It includes many notes that will help you understand the text you're reading. Books giving a good Catholic explanation of the Bible are also useful. These resources can help you understand what it means to be part of the Catholic Church. Spend time (outside of prayer time) familiarizing yourself with the Bible and using your Bible in prayer. But be patient. Learning takes time.

The Bible is a compilation of smaller books and is not meant to be read in a continuous, front-to-back manner. In the text, you will find subheadings. Focus on one section during your prayer time. Ask the Holy Spirit to reveal to you the mysteries hidden in the text. Start by reading one of the Gospels. The Gospel of Mark was the first Gospel written and is a good starting point.

Considering the following questions about the text you are reading will enhance your understanding:

1. What does it say?
2. What does it mean?
3. How do I apply it in my life?

Remember, the Holy Spirit is your guide and teacher. Ask Him for help with passages you do not understand or for the meaning of a particular text. Trust that the Holy Spirit will do this. He will also provide other disciples who are further along in their journey to help you with questions you may have.

Once you have finished reading the Gospel of Mark, ask the Holy Spirit to lead you to the next book in the Bible to read.

☙❧

The Breaking of the Bread

If we do not have Jesus living in our hearts, through the powerful indwelling of the Holy Spirit, we will not be able to recognize Jesus in the Eucharist. Why? It is this encounter with God in our hearts that enables us to see that his word is true and worthy of embracing in our lives. This encounter enables us to be properly disposed in faith to the Lord's coming in the Blessed Sacrament during Mass.

When you spend time with someone you become familiar with them and their presence. The same is true with the Holy Spirit. You encounter that wonderful fruit of peace that cannot be generated any other way than to be in a right relationship with God. It is this familiarity that helps us learn to trust in the Church's teaching of the Mass and to recognize the Lord's presence in the Eucharist.

Eat My Flesh, Drink My Blood

In the Gospel of John, chapter six, we have the "bread of life" narrative. In this text, Jesus lays the ground work for the Mass by describing how we must eat his flesh and drink his blood to have life within us (John 6:53, NRSV).

Jesus had just fed five thousand people the day before. The crowd, hoping for more free food, follows Jesus across the sea. When Jesus sees them, he confronts their motive for following him. Jesus encourages them not to work for food that perishes, but for food that will endure for eternal life (John 6:27). The crowd asks what they must do to work for God. Jesus' response is very clear -- their work for God is to believe in Jesus. *He is calling them to authentic faith.*

After responding to a request for a sign, like Moses gave their ancestors manna in the desert, Jesus makes a proclamation they struggled to understand -- "I am the Bread of Life" (John 6:35, NRSV). In clarifying his statement, Jesus intensifies the confusion. "I am the living bread that came down from heaven. Whoever eats of this bread will live forever; and the bread that I will give for the life of the world is *my flesh*" (John 6:51, NRSV; emphasis added). Can Jesus really be talking about his own literal flesh? There are many books on the Mass to help believers understand it better. I encourage you to study any of these books to acquire a thorough understanding of the significance of the Mass.

Many of the disciples who were following Jesus found his words to be so difficult to believe that they walked away. If Jesus was only speaking figuratively, why did he let them go? If they simply misunderstood his meaning, wouldn't Jesus have corrected that? It is precisely because his words were true that he let them go. Jesus was not asking them to fully understand how the bread was his body, the wine his blood. He was asking them to trust him and calling them to deepen their faith. Just because they could not yet understand Jesus' teaching did not mean it was not true.

The Lord's Supper

It is not until Holy Thursday, at the Lord's Supper, commonly called the Last Supper, that we hear of this reference to his body and blood again. At the Passover Feast, Jesus is the "Rabbi," leading the Passover ritual (liturgy). When he offers bread for the Apostles to eat he defines it as his flesh (Matthew 26:26). He offers the wine as his blood, the blood of a new covenant.

Under the old covenant the Israelites took a lamb, sacrificed it, cooked it, and consumed it. This Passover covenant enabled them to avoid the angel of death and live. The new covenant Jesus spoke of was not replacing the old, but fulfilling it. Jesus is the Passover lamb who was sacrificed for the world. This explains why he left in the middle of the Passover celebration with his Apostles without concluding the ritual (Matthew 26:30). They needed to sing the hymns, drink from the cup a fourth time and then say the concluding words.

Prior to departing the Passover Liturgy, Jesus speaks into reality the sacrifice that atones for the sins of all of humanity. His atoning sacrifice began when he transformed the bread and wine into his Body, Blood, Soul and Divinity and offered it up for the sins of the world. The passion and death of the Lord is the conclusion of the Passover Feast. While on the cross, Jesus drinks the vinegar wine (fourth cup) offered by the Roman and then recites the concluding words of the

Passover Sacrifice – "It is finished"! (John 19:30, NRSV) (Theological interpretation gleaned from Dr. Scott Hahn's Audio Presentation Entitled The Fourth Cup)

The real Passover not only freed the Israelites from the bondage of slavery under the Egyptians but also frees us from the bondage of sin.

The Eternal Sacrifice

What the Orthodox Jews celebrate once a year is the same thing that we Catholics celebrate daily, the eternal sacrifice of the Lamb of God. The Early Church understood, from the very beginning, that when they gathered at the breaking of the bread, they were sharing the body of Christ given for all eternity. It is not a retelling of a story, but a portal (of sorts) to return to the original event. When the Mass is said, we are brought to the very sacrifice that gains our freedom. We are brought to the foot of the cross. It is here that we regain perspective on why we give our lives to Jesus.

The Wedding Feast of the Lamb

The Mass is also the time when the Groom (Jesus) takes his Bride (the Church) in marriage. In the wedding feast of the Lamb of God (Revelations 19), the Groom presents his Bride to his Heavenly Father. In the Mass, we are taken to the throne room of God and presented to him as holy and pure. It is in this marital union that we are united with God and able to share in his divine life. The Mass is not only the Lord's wedding day, but ours too. If this is true, then how do we prepare for this sacred union with God? Are we prayerful? How should we dress? Do we approach the Mass with expectation of union with God? These are all areas where we can ask the Holy Spirit for guidance as we continue our journey of faith.

Home Base

Mass is like the "home base" often used in the game of tag. Players anxiously leave home base and try to avoid the person who is "it." When the person who is "it" gets dangerously close, the players flee from them and run back to the safety of the base. All the players know where the base is and are always conscious of how far away they are from it.

The Mass should always be our point of reference, our home base. Our new identity in Christ flows from the Sacrifice of the Mass. It is there that we have gained our freedom from sin. It is there that we have gained our new identity as adopted children of God. It is there that we receive Jesus' true body, like a bride on her wedding night, into our bodies and become one flesh.

All the other sacraments are uniquely connected to the Mass. God's graces flow through every sacrament because of this sacrament of love and sacrifice. When our faith deepens and we freely enter into this relationship, we will do all that is necessary to remain in union with God. In the development of this fundamental discipline, it is vital to study Scripture and Church teachings to understand how each Sacrament is connected to the Eucharist.

Engaging the Discipline of Breaking the Bread

We can sit back and say we're only required to go to Mass once a week because that is acceptable according to the "rules" of the Church. However, a mature disciple desiring to draw closer to the Lord strives to attend Mass as frequently as possible. To recognize the Lord's true presence in the Blessed Sacrament requires one to choose to believe in Jesus' word and act on it. The Lord is truly present to us every day in the Mass. Faith enables us to dispose our hearts to the Lord at this sacred feast and gain the graces needed to go out and live the truth. Mass attendance becomes no longer just an obligation, but rather a result of one's desire to be intimately close to our Lord. Being prayerfully and sacramentally (Confession when needed) prepared for Mass becomes a priority. A mature disciple longs to be present with the Lord and leave the feast encouraged and renewed in their faith.

Ask the Holy Spirit to help you better understand the Mass and its centrality to our Catholic Faith. Ask the Spirit to help you properly dispose your heart so that you can give it to Him at every Mass. Go to Mass with the Holy Spirit, being attentive to everything going on and listen to the instructions of the Lord while you are there. Finally, expect to be renewed in faith, hope, and love. You will be strengthened to go out and live the truth of Jesus' words.

࿎

Final Notes

This book is designed to help you get started in your new life with Jesus Christ in the Catholic Church. If you are serious about establishing a solid relationship with Him—and not letting Satan and his army separate you from God for eternity—it is vital that you intentionally grow your faith through Scripture study (understanding), daily prayer (communication with Jesus), disposing yourself to the true presence of Jesus in the sacraments, and becoming an active member in the community of the body of Christ in its service to its members and the world.

Small Groups

The first-century Church included fellowship as one of the four pillars of faith. Being a committed disciple of Christ requires much more than joining a church and becoming a faithful member. Participation in a small group provides an intimate gathering where you can commit to study, sharing, and growth with other believers. Group members can share struggles and success stories, discuss the faith, and talk about how their faith has manifested itself in their lives. Through small groups, disciples grow to care about and invest themselves in each other, individually and as a group.

Becoming part of a small group should be a priority as soon as possible after your conversion. And remember, every disciple has been where you are now.

If you are reading this material following a Parish Mission, seek out three to five others who are also committed to their faith and begin meeting weekly. During your meetings, allow every person to share how they are doing in their disciplines. Being part of a group will strengthen you against attacks of the enemy, add accountability to your efforts, and accelerate the growth of your faith. A small group is successful only if those involved are willing to be honest about their journey. Playing "Christian" and pretending you are doing perfectly well won't reap fruit for anyone.

Warning! Well over fifty percent of new believers who don't follow up their conversion by joining a group find their faith attacked and fall away. Remember, it is Satan's goal to separate you from God for eternity.

If you have purchased this book on your own, please look for a few other people you might invite to join you in this journey (either one-on-one or in a group) or contact your parish staff for guidance and support.

The Holy Spirit
Get to know the Holy Spirit. At the start of every day, invite Him to come into your life. Ask Him to be

your teacher and guide. He lives in you and is waiting for an invitation to become an active part of your life. Learn how to include the Spirit in your life.

Spiritual Director

Find a mature disciple of Christ to help you grow closer to the Lord. Ask that person to meet with you regularly to review your progress, explain the teachings of the Bible, provide encouragement, and hold you accountable in your journey.

Discipleship Card

On the last page of this book, find the Discipleship Card, which was created to help you in your growth. Place the card on your bathroom mirror or anywhere else that will be visible to you daily. Let it be a reminder of the commitment you made to Jesus and a record of your progress. At the bottom of the card is a brief but powerful prayer you can say each morning as you get ready to start your day.

[Hint: *Before using the card, make extra copies for future use.*]

LEARNING HOW TO DIE TO SELF
Discipleship Disciplines
Mirror Card

Mark an **X** on days you have your **quiet time**.	**X = Quiet Time**
Draw a **circle** on dates for **Mass attendance**.	**O = Mass**
Draw a **square** for **Reconciliation reception**.	**□ = Reconciliation**
Underline dates of **small Group meetings**.	**— = Small Group**

Month 1

   1 2 3 4 5 6 7 8 9 10 11 12 13 14 15 16
17 18 19 20 21 22 23 24 25 26 27 28 29 30 31

Month 2

   1 2 3 4 5 6 7 8 9 10 11 12 13 14 15 16
17 18 19 20 21 22 23 24 25 26 27 28 29 30 31

Month 3

   1 2 3 4 5 6 7 8 9 10 11 12 13 14 15 16
17 18 19 20 21 22 23 24 25 26 27 28 29 30 31

Month 4

   1 2 3 4 5 6 7 8 9 10 11 12 13 14 15 16
17 18 19 20 21 22 23 24 25 26 27 28 29 30 31

Month 5

   1 2 3 4 5 6 7 8 9 10 11 12 13 14 15 16
17 18 19 20 21 22 23 24 25 26 27 28 29 30 31

Month 6

   1 2 3 4 5 6 7 8 9 10 11 12 13 14 15 16
17 18 19 20 21 22 23 24 25 26 27 28 29 30 31

Heavenly Father, in the name of Jesus Christ, send your Holy Spirit to lead me today. Amen.